The World of Work

Choosing a Career in Banking and Finance

There are a wide range of careers in the field of banking and finance.

The World of Work

Choosing a Career in Banking and Finance

Carolyn Simpson

THE ROSEN PUBLISHING GROUP, INC.

NEW YORK

Published in 1997 by The Rosen Publishing Group, Inc.
29 East 21st Street, New York, NY 10010

First Edition

Library of Congress Cataloging-in-Publication Data

Simpson, Carolyn.
    Choosing a career in banking and finance/Carolyn Simpson.
      p.   cm.—(The World of work)
    Includes bibliographical references and index.
    Summary: Offers an overview of careers in finance-related fields, discussing required education, salaries and other potential rewards, as well as drawbacks.
    ISBN 0-8239-2269-3
    1. Banks and banking—Vocational guidance—United States—Juvenile literature. 2. Finance—Vocational guidance—United States—Juvenile literature. [1. Banks and banking—Vocational guidance. 2. Finance—Vocational guidance. 3. Vocational guidance.]
I. Title. II. Series: The World of work (New York, N.Y.)
HG1609.S56   1996
332.1′023′73—dc20   96-14323
                                                 CIP
                                                   AC

Manufactured in the United States of America

Contents

Introduction

Banks have been around since ancient times. In fact, a bank called the Igibi existed in Babylon twenty-five hundred years ago. It performed many of the same services as modern banks: taking deposits, paying and charging interest, and making loans. Banks have come a long way since then. ATMS (automated teller machines) have partly replaced human tellers. People don't even have to handle real money anymore. Checks can be written for many of their purchases. They can even have their employer deposit their paychecks directly into their bank accounts, which is called a *direct deposit*.

Banks exist for two basic reasons:
1. To provide a safe place to keep and invest money.
2. To provide a source for borrowing money.

Banks bring together people who need money and people who have money to lend.

People who work in banks need to be able to keep accurate records of all transactions.

To be successful in banking, you must be able to work well with your coworkers and customers.

People who lend money don't just lend it to any customer who walks through their front door. Loan officers first need to figure out which people are likely to repay the loans and which ones are not.

Banks also need people to keep accurate records. Still others are needed to check those records to make sure that the bank is not mishandling its money.

In the past, banks concentrated on making their profit on the *spread*. The spread is the difference between the interest that banks pay on savings accounts and the interest they charge on loans. Today banks make money in many different ways. Trust account officers make money for banks by managing people's properties. Financial planners make money for banks by giving advice to customers about how to invest their money.

The bank employee of the future is someone who understands all the details about his or her bank, but also sees the bigger picture. He or she is someone who knows where his bank fits into the community and who plans to keep it competitive with all the other banks.

Questions to Ask Yourself

Banks and other financial institutions may seem complicated and confusing. But if you look at their basic parts, it becomes easier to understand their purposes and uses. 1) What are the two basic reasons that banks exist? 2) Who are the people that are most likely to receive loans?

Banks employ loan officers and accountants as well as tellers.

The Basics About the World of Finance   1

There are many kinds of banks and other financial institutions. *Consumer banks* serve individuals and small businesses. *Commercial banks* serve larger businesses and institutions. Both offer a full range of services, including savings accounts, checking accounts, loans, safe-deposit boxes, investment planning, and travelers checks.

Savings and loan associations (S&Ls) are similar to consumer banks except that they specialize in all types of saving accounts and home mortgage loans. *Mortgage companies* specialize in lending money to buy houses and business property.

Finance companies help the person who needs a small personal loan. Their interest rates are often higher than those of banks.

Finally, *credit unions* are nonprofit groups that work like savings and loan associations. Credit unions are owned by the people who deposit money into them.

The jobs described in the next chapters are all related to these financial institutions. Most places have *tellers*—the employees who handle the actual money during a transaction between a person and the institution. They also employ loan officers, accountants, and auditors. In finance companies and mortgage companies, however, the duties of some employees overlap with the duties of others.

In smaller banks, employees tend to be *generalists*. They need to know a little about a lot of things. At larger banks, employees tend to be *specialists*. They need to know a lot about a few special things. At a small bank, two or more jobs may be the responsibility of one person. At a larger bank several people would do those tasks.

There's no description of a typical "banker" because bankers don't exist. Instead there are many people with different responsibilities within a bank: auditors and accountants, tellers and administrative assistants, loan officers and financial planners.

What Skills and Qualities Do I Need?

Banks seek to hire people with certain skills and qualities.

All bank employees must have *integrity*,

which means being honest, responsible, and dependable. No matter what the job is, you're working with other people's money. The bank needs to know that you can be trusted with it.

Employees need to be *efficient* and *detail-oriented*. Small details can be important. Tellers must be able to handle transactions with customers quickly but accurately. Credit analysts and accountants need to pay close attention to what they're doing in order to avoid costly errors as well.

Employees need to be *personable* because they work directly with the public. Even auditors and accountants work with people, so it pays to have a friendly attitude. Tellers especially need to be personable because they are usually the customer's first contact with a bank. If they make a poor impression, the bank risks losing a customer. They also need to be *diplomatic* because they are called upon to handle customer complaints or demands in a courteous and respectful way.

Employees need to be able to maintain *confidentiality*. This means that you respect the privacy of your customers' financial business and do not reveal it to anyone else. By working in a financial institution, you'll learn a lot about other people's finances.

Customers count on you not to discuss their business with others.

Employees should be *calm* and *resourceful*. They may have to deal with an angry customer who has been turned down for a loan, or to ask a disorderly customer to leave the building. They may catch a person passing a counterfeit bill or a forged check. Employees can handle the situation better if they don't give in to panic.

Finally, anyone who wants to work in a financial institution should have a good understanding of math, accounting, bookkeeping, and business. They should have excellent written and oral communication skills. They should enjoy working with numbers. It's helpful to know how to use calculators, adding machines, and computers, but those skills can be learned on the job. Employees must be willing to learn as new technology is developed.

Questions to Ask Yourself

There is a lot to learn about financial institutions. 1) What are the types of banks and financial institutions? 2) Why do employees in financial institutions need to be detail-oriented? 3) Are you detail-oriented?

Entry-Level Jobs

2

The following job descriptions have specific titles, but not every bank calls the jobs by the same name. As a rule, larger banks have more people doing different jobs. Smaller banks combine some of the duties and perhaps give a new title to the job. When you check job opportunities at individual financial institutions, you will be able to see what job titles each uses.

Ted, Bank Teller

Ted worked as a bank teller one summer. His days were always different. One day a little girl and her mother came to his teller window. The little girl handed Ted a big plastic bag filled with pennies. "Could you change this into dollars?" she asked.

Ted smiled. He remembered when he was young. He had to count the pennies himself and put them into penny rolls before his bank would accept them. How much easier it was now just to keep it all in a plastic bag.

"It'll just take a minute," Ted said. "I'm going to pour your pennies into a machine that will count them for us."

Ted emptied the bag into the machine. The little girl laughed as she heard her coins tumbling down the slot. When the counting stopped, Ted looked at the amount and handed her five crisp dollar bills. "There you go," he said. "And how about a lollipop, if your mom thinks it's okay?"

The little girl looked at her mother, who nodded. As she clasped her bills and the lollipop, her mother smiled at Ted. "Thanks for being so nice," she said.

The next man in line wanted to borrow some money on his credit card. Ted handled the transaction easily once the man provided identification and his credit card.

Another man wanted to pay his electric bill. He handed Ted the money and bill. That was also an easy transaction.

The last person in line was an elderly woman who approached Ted's window hesitantly. She took a wrinkled Social Security check from her purse. She asked Ted if he'd cash it for her. Ted noticed that she seemed to have a lot of money loose in her purse. He worried about her purse being stolen.

"I'll be glad to cash that check for you," he said. "But have you ever thought of opening a checking account? Then you wouldn't have to carry around so much cash."

The woman thought for a moment. "Oh, it's too much trouble to balance a checkbook," she said.

"Well, I could introduce you to one of our account representatives. He can help you open an account and show you how to use it. Besides," Ted added, "you could have the government deposit your checks directly into your account each month. You wouldn't even have to come down to the bank."

The woman thought about Ted's suggestion some more. "That's not a bad idea," she said.

"Let me take you over to meet our account representative, Mr. Harkins. He'll take the time to explain our checking accounts."

The woman thanked Ted. Later that day the bank manager stopped by to tell Ted that he'd done a good job by helping the woman in a way that also benefited the bank.

That afternoon, Ted was working the drive-through window. A man handed Ted a check to cash. When Ted checked the account, he

A bank teller deals directly with customers.

discovered there wasn't enough money to pay the check. Ted felt awkward because he knew the man would probably be embarrassed.

"I'm sorry, sir, I can't cash this check just yet. You don't have sufficient funds to cover it," he said.

"Well, I'll be making a deposit later this afternoon," the man said. "But I need the money right now."

"I'm sorry. I can't do that," Ted said. "But perhaps you could step inside and speak to our manager, Mrs. Edwards."

The man looked uncomfortable. "What can she do?"

"Well, for one thing, you could ask her about a special kind of checking account called a reserve checking account. It would cover any checks overdrawn on your account. Or you could apply for a bank credit card."

"Okay," the man said. "I'll park and be right in."

"I'll tell her to expect you," Ted said, reaching for the phone.

At the end of the day, Ted began the process of settling. Settling meant that he had to make sure that the amount of money listed on the receipts from the day's transactions was the same as the amount he had in his register. Some *days it was easier than others. One time he had to stay forty-five minutes extra to find an error. That time, he'd written $45 instead of $54. It had taken him that long to realize that he had switched the numbers.*

Today, Ted was only twenty-five cents short. He sighed. "Hey, just throw in a quarter," another teller suggested.

"It'll mess things up," Ted said. "Someone else will find the error, and then I'll be twenty-five cents over."

Ted looked through his drawer again. "Wait a minute," he exclaimed, picking out the quarter. "Here it is." He smiled as he marked "OK" on his worksheets. Now he was ready to leave for the day.

As you can see from Ted's experiences, a bank teller handles many different tasks. He or she makes deposits and withdrawals, cashes checks and accepts loan payments. He also checks for torn or damaged bills and counterfeit money. He suggests additional services to customers and has to settle all his transactions at the end of the day.

The position of bank teller is an entry-level job. The starting salary ranges between $10,500 and $24,300 per year. One of the good things about the teller position is that there are always job openings and part-time opportunities. Banks provide excellent benefits, including lower interest rates on loans and free checking accounts. They also provide free in-service training, medical and dental benefits, and payment for additional classes in business-related subjects.

Account Representative

Through additional training, bank tellers can move on to become *account representatives*. Account representatives make a little more money than tellers because they have additional responsibilities. In addition to filling in for the tellers, they must be familiar with all the bank services. Since their main job is to sell services to the new customer, they must explain these services to the customer in a clear and convincing way.

Account representatives set up both checking and savings accounts. They sell certificates of deposit and money market accounts. To invest in a *certificate of deposit*, or CD, a customer deposits a certain amount of money into the bank and agrees not to withdraw it for three months, six months, a year, or more. The bank, which has the use of

An account representative helps people set up the type of bank accounts that fulfill their needs.

this money, pays the customer an interest rate that depends on the term of the CD. The longer the customer agrees to keep his or her money in the bank, the higher the rate of interest. *Money market accounts* are similar to checking accounts. A person can write a check that draws money from his money market account. But the money in the account is invested in mutual funds and stocks. The bank keeps some of the money it earns from the investing. The customer keeps the rest.

An account representative can also arrange for a security or safe-deposit box where a person can place valuables or important papers.

Branch Manager

Branch managers usually earn a salary of $30,000 or more. Larger banks have branch offices located in other towns. Branch managers act as Chief Executive Officers, or CEOs, for these branches. Their duties may include setting up accounts, arranging and approving loans, and dealing with customer complaints. They oversee the daily operation of the bank and its employees, and open the bank in the mornings.

Support Staff and Data Processors

Many other people are needed to help the bank to function.

Secretaries type correspondence, answer phones, schedule appointments and meetings, order supplies, and distribute mail.

Administrative assistants are like secretaries but have added responsibilities. They might fill out certain documents, make travel arrangements, and keep accurate records for administration.

File clerks maintain accurate and up-to-date files. They file and retrieve documents as

An accounting clerk may research statistics or assist the head accountant in other ways.

needed, and put old records on microfilm. Other clerks perform word processing and record keeping as needed.

Loan clerks process customers' applications for loans. They help the bank decide who is likely to pay back a loan and who is not.

Accounting clerks handle billing and payroll duties. They may also assist accountants in researching statistics for documents.

Maintenance workers are responsible for keeping the building clean and well-supplied. They may also attend to the area outside the bank or financial institution. They must be responsible and dependable and be able to follow assignments without constant supervision.

In *clerical jobs*, candidates need to have an eye for detail as well as good typing and spelling skills. It is also important to be able to use certain office equipment, such as a typewriter or word processor and printer, photocopier, and fax machine. Courtesy, friendliness, and politeness are essential skills, especially when working with the public and other personnel. Above all, the clerical staff needs to be able to keep the information they learn at the bank confidential.

Data processors earn from $17,000 to

$25,000 depending on the size of the bank or financial institution. They enter all data on a person's account into the computer. The data processor needs a good understanding of computers and data processing. These skills are usually taught in high school or technical schools.

Questions to Ask Yourself

Many entry-level positions are available in the world of banks and financial institutions.
1) What are some of the skills and qualities that you need to work in a bank? 2) Do you have some or all of these skills? If so, which ones? 3) If not, how can you learn some of these skills?

Working Your Way Up 3

*M*onique wanted to be a bank vice president someday, but she knew her parents couldn't afford to pay for her college. She didn't think that her grades were good enough to win a full scholarship either. So she thought she could begin her career working as a bank teller, but she didn't know how to move up from that position without going to college.

One day she mentioned her financial situation to a friend whose father worked in a bank. "I want to work my way to the top, but I don't think I can do it without a college degree."

Her friend, Harmony, looked surprised. "My dad is a vice president at his bank. And he doesn't have a college degree."

"Well, then, he must be related to the bank president or something," Monique said.

"No, he's not."

"You mean that you don't need any college experience for such a high-level position?"

"Most people need a college degree to move up the career ladder. But sometimes you can work your way up. My dad started out as a mail clerk, sorting mail and taking it around to the various departments. It was a good job for someone just out of high school."

"But can a mail clerk really become a vice president in charge of loans?" Monique asked.

"Not unless he shows some ability," Harmony explained. "You see, the bank offers courses in banking procedures. Dad got interested in other aspects of banking, such as loans. He took a few night courses at the local college, and the bank paid for them. He learned a lot from those finance and accounting courses."

"So you're saying that you can pick up some education along the way?"

"Of course, but that's not all. Dad was willing to work hard. He didn't go from being a mail clerk to a vice president. He spent quite a few years learning other jobs first. In fact, he's worked at the bank for nineteen years."

Monique was starting to feel a lot better about her future. "Wow, I thought you had to have a college degree before you could even think about getting a job in a bank."

There are several ways to reach the important position of manager of a bank.

Harmony smiled. "Well, a college degree is helpful, but hard work and a lot of learning along the way can go just as far."

There are four ways you can work your way up in the world of finance: management training, in-service training, flexibility and dedication, and luck. Management training requires that you have a college degree. The others do not.

Management Training

A person can begin training as a manager right out of college. This means that your "entry-level job" is a special program.

In-Service Training

Once you have a job at a bank, you can attend *in-service training* seminars. Most banks offer employees free courses in the various aspects of banking. All you have to do is show your interest in learning.

Most banks also offer to pay the tuition of employees who take college courses in business-related subjects and do well. The American Institute of Business is the educational branch of the American Bankers Association (ABA). They offer courses to ABA members in accounting, economics, marketing, investment, finance, and business administration, to name just a few.

So even if you don't start with all the technical skills and knowledge you need for your job, you can learn them while you work, as Harmony's dad did.

Flexibility and Dedication

Flexibility and dedication are key factors in moving up to positions of higher responsibility. Sometimes people have to be willing to move to another bank. You may limit your chances by staying in one location, especially if your bank has several branches around the state. Dedication means working hard, which for some people means putting in long hours. The person who puts a 100 percent effort into her job will be noticed, as long as her work is accurate.

Luck
Finally, there's always luck. Sometimes you just happen to be in the right place at the right time to be chosen for the job.

Many Opportunities
Once you are employed at a bank, there are many opportunities for you to advance. The following chapter will discuss positions in the world of finance that require additional skills or training. If you set your mind to it, you can go far.

Questions to Ask Yourself
It is not necessary to have a college degree to begin a career in banking. 1) How could you work yourself up from an entry-level position? 2) Would you be willing to take a few evening courses in banking subjects? 3) Why do you think banks have in-service training seminars? How does the bank benefit?

Jobs such as credit analyst require more training than the bank can provide.

Jobs That Require Greater Specialization 4

Banks also employ accountants, auditors, credit analysts, financial planners, trust officers, loan officers, lawyers, and human resource officers. These jobs require *greater specialization*, which usually means having taken college courses and often means having a college degree. However, many people make up for the lack of a college degree with years of banking experience and in-service training. Some bank executives, like Harmony's dad, climbed to the top without earning a college degree. It is certainly possible to do, but it is very difficult because so many people with college degrees are competing for the limited number of available jobs.

In short, it makes sense to get as much college education as you can. However, an employee who has worked hard for many years with a bank and taken courses in accounting and finance may have many opportunities as well.

If you do go to college, you don't necessarily have to go to a business college or even to major in business administration (although either option is fine). As long as you take courses in business, accounting, finance, and economics, you can major in whatever you want. Banks often prefer employees with a well-rounded or liberal arts background. These students have been exposed to many different subjects. Majors might include history, psychology, sociology, or English.

Denise, Bank Intern

Denise spent the summer between her junior and senior years in college as a bank intern. Even though she was studying to be an accountant, she worked in each of the departments in the bank.

The first couple of weeks, she was with the tellers, learning how they handled things. The next couple of weeks she worked with a loan officer. After that she helped the credit analysts.

Erin, her roommate from college, called her one evening. "How's the job going?" she asked.

"Wow, I had no idea banking was so complicated," Denise said.

"How can it be complicated?" Erin asked. "All a bank does is open checking accounts and make loans."

"Oh, banks do much more than that. Besides, do you know how complicated it is to make a loan?"

"How is a loan complicated?" Erin asked. "You just put down how much money you need, say what you need it for, and the bank checks your credit. If you've got good credit, you get the loan."

"It's not quite that simple," Denise said. "The person may have good credit but may already have too many loans out. He may not be able to pay this loan back because he has too much debt. A good credit analyzer checks out all the risks possible. He advises the loan officer."

"Okay, so loans are a little more involved. Maybe banks need a few credit analysts along with the loan officers."

"Well, banks need to know if they have enough money to lend, too," Denise said. "That's where accountants help. And what if the bank is mismanaging its money? Spotting that is an auditor's job."

"You mean someone might be stealing money?"

"Maybe," Denise said. "But it's also possible that a teller is secretly borrowing money from the drawer and plans to pay it back on payday. A surprise audit would catch that."

"It sounds like you're not having a boring summer at all," Erin said, surprised.

"I'm not," Denise said. "In fact, sometimes this doesn't feel like work at all. You know what the best part is? I will have all this experience when I apply for a real job next year."

For the following jobs, it's not enough to have a good working knowledge of math, bookkeeping, and computers. You also need to have an understanding of tax laws, bank regulations, and investment planning. You'll be called upon to advise people about how to invest their money.

Accountants, Auditors, and Controllers

People who fill auditor and accounting positions in a bank may both be accountants, but the focus of each job is different. Both make between $25,000 and $65,000 (depending on the size of their bank and their job responsibilities).

Accountants monitor how well the bank is earning its money. They write reports, keep accurate financial records, and prepare budgets. To be an accountant, you need a license. To get a license, you need to pass a state exam to become a *Public Accountant* (PA). Every year after having earned a license, the PA must complete a certain number of hours of professional education and pay a fee to keep the license.

To become a *Certified Public Accountant* (CPA), the candidate must pass an exam given by the American Institute of Certified Public Accountants. This exam has four parts. You will have to pass all four parts. If you don't, you will have to re-take it. After passing the entire exam, the candidate must work for other accountants for two years before starting his own practice.

Many states are now trying to get rid of the PA title and recognize only CPAS. Some states require 150 hours of college coursework before a student can take the CPA exam. This amounts to an additional year of college beyond the bachelor's degree.

An *auditor* checks the bank's records. She sees if the records are accurate and looks for any evidence of mismanagement of funds, including *embezzlement*, or theft of money. Tellers' cash boxes are sometimes checked by the auditor to see whether their transactions and record keeping are accurate. It is also the responsibility of the auditor to review the company's operations and evaluate how well it's doing. She must see if the bank's policies and procedures are properly followed.

The difference between the accountant and the auditor is that the accountant prepares the reports and books, and the auditor checks them over.

Controllers oversee the accounting and budget departments (and sometimes the auditing department). They earn between $44,000 and $100,000, depending on the size of the bank.

Credit Analysts and Loan Officers

In smaller banks, there isn't much difference between credit analysts and loan officers.

In larger financial institutions, the *loan officer* makes out the loan application and discusses it with the customer. The *credit analyst* researches the credit information to determine if the customer has good credit. He approves or rejects the loan based on what he finds. The loan officer then reports the

A loan officer works with customers who have loans. She makes sure they pay on time, and that they meet the terms of the loan.

information found by the credit analyst to the customer. If the loan has been approved, he may *service* the loan. This means that he may accept payments from the customer and follow up when payments are late. The loan officer may also renegotiate the terms of the loan agreement.

Loan officers earn between $25,000 and $48,000. Credit analysts earn between $35,000 and $50,000.

Financial Planners and Trust Officers

Financial planners and trust officers both take care of their customers' money. They often give advice about how to invest money as well as handling a customer's investments.

A *financial planner* focuses on advising a client about how to save and manage money for the future. He comes up with plans for managing property, saving for a child's education or saving for a retirement fund. He might even suggest ways to save on taxes. After meeting with the client, the financial planner can explain the various ways a client can save money to plan for the future.

A *trust officer* may actually handle the investments of his client. He may also take care of a client's property or guarantee that the instructions on a client's will are properly followed. He is usually given the authority to act in the customer's best interest.

Both of these employees can be paid in several different ways. Some employees work strictly on *commission*. This means that they earn a percentage of the profit made from their investments of a client's money. Others work for a set fee that depends on the service they provide the customer with. Some work for a base salary and also earn a commission if the customer follows their suggestions and invests in the bank's services.

Bank lawyers make sure that banks follow the laws that apply to each transaction.

Lawyers

Lawyers are needed to make sure that all transactions between the bank and a client are done legally. Lawyers know which laws apply to each business transaction. They advise the bank about how to act in various situations. For example, sometimes a bank's client will fail to make payments on a loan. If this happens, the bank is protected by a business agreement known as *collateral*. In this agreement, the client agrees to give up some of his property to the bank to cover the unpaid loan. Lawyers take care of the details involved in taking the property.

If banks don't have their own lawyers on staff, they use lawyers from a local company. Lawyers need four years of college and three additional years of law school. Then they must pass the bar exam for the state in which they want to practice law. Law is a high-paying profession.

Human Resources

The people in *human resources* handle the hiring and firing of employees. They also take care of employee benefits. Some may also hold seminars for employees.

The human resources department also has the important responsibility of making sure that their financial institution respects equal opportunity laws. This means that the opportunity to work is granted to an individual on the basis of his or her ability. Equal opportunity laws do not allow an employer to discriminate against someone because of such factors as race, sex, or age. The human resource department also handles complaints and problems with sexual harassment.

Depending on the size of the bank, the

human resources department may require the help of clerks and secretaries. Applicants for human resources positions often need some college experience in human resources. Experience in banking can be substituted for a college degree in some cases, depending on the institution.

Bank Executives

The *Chief Executive Officer* (CEO) and *Chief Financial Officer* (CFO) of a bank are usually the top two people in the organization. These executives have usually climbed the corporate ladder, often starting as loan officers, accountants, credit analysts, auditors, or trust officers. They have the highest status in the organization and make the most money. They are also responsible for the overall performance of the bank and its employees. As always, the larger the salary the greater the responsibility.

Questions to Ask Yourself

Many of the jobs in banks require some level of higher education. 1) What are some of the courses you should take in college to help you prepare for such jobs? 2) What are some of those types of jobs?

Most of the money that is deposited in a bank is insured by the FDIC.

The Future of Banking 5

*J*anet and Manuel were working on a joint paper for English class. Since they both wanted to get into the banking and finance industry, they'd chosen to write about banking. Manuel looked up from his notes.

"You know, Janet," he said. "The only thing wrong with banks is that they're so unstable."

"Unstable!" Janet said. "Banks haven't been unstable since the Great Depression. Their money is protected by the Federal Deposit Insurance Corporation (FDIC). That insures a depositor's money for up to $100,000 on each account in case there is a bank robbery or the bank goes out of business."

"I don't mean unstable in that sense," he said. "I mean that nowadays banks seem to be merging all the time and that makes people's jobs unstable. For example, say someone gets to be the CEO of his bank. Before he knows it, a bigger bank comes along and merges with his bank. Next thing he knows, he isn't the CEO *anymore and has been moved to another position of lesser responsibility. A lot of people lose their jobs when banks are taken over by a bigger bank."*

"I see what you mean," Janet said. "Bank mergers are likely to be a thing of the future since banks are so competitive."

"Think of getting to be Executive Vice President and then losing your job," Manuel objected. "That would be terrible."

"I'd say that's bad, but other jobs are out there," Janet replied.

"Well, who wants to be looking for a job again after ten years with a bank?"

"Someone who needs another job," Janet answered, matter-of-factly. "Look, my uncle works in a bank. He says bank mergers happen more and more often. This forces the smart employee to keep his skills sharp."

"What does he mean?" asked Manuel.

"Well, the smart employee takes courses that the bank offers in accounting, auditing, or bank procedures. He will also learn as much as he can about computers. If he loses one job, he'll have good enough skills to compete for others."

"Yes, but how will he find out about these other jobs?"

"My uncle says that the smart employee keeps networking even after he has a job," Janet said.

"What's networking?"

"It's when you make contacts with others in your line of work and stay in touch with them. Most of us have friends who have friends in various businesses. If you asked those contacts, you'd learn of job openings sooner or later."

"So your uncle is a potential contact for me right now."

"Sure," Janet said. *"He'd be glad to talk to you if you mentioned you were friends with me."*

"So networking keeps me aware of the job openings out there?"

"Yes, and you can network by talking with friends from church, school, or even in your neighborhood. Joining organizations puts you in touch with a lot of people who might be good contacts."

"Let me see if I've got this right," Manuel said. *"If an employee keeps his skills up and networks well, he shouldn't have trouble finding another job."*

"Well, there's one other thing," Janet said. *"Someone who wants to get a new job or keep*

As the banking industry continues to grow, so will the need for employees.

an existing one needs to be flexible. He may need to move to a different city; he may even have to switch jobs. If he's willing to consider moving or changing jobs, he'll probably survive any merger. Banks prefer experienced people."

"This talk has left me feeling more and more confident about getting a job in a bank in the future," Manuel said, smiling. "Did you get any other advice?"

"As a matter of fact, I did," Janet said. "One of the loan officers at my uncle's bank told me to always be nice to people. If you're considerate of others, they will be considerate of you. And who knows, they might even do you a favor when you need one."

The banking and finance industry, like many other industries, is in a time of great change as a result of the technological revolution. Almost every procedure in various fields, from manufacturing to publishing, has changed because of new technology. This is especially true in banking. New laws are expected soon that will allow banks in one city to have branches in cities across the country. This will mean not only the expansion of business, but also the expansion of the number of bank employees.

All these changes will make it even more important for bank employees to keep up their skills and learn new ones. They must be ready when an unexpected opportunity—or a job that never existed before—comes within their reach.

Questions to Ask Yourself

Opportunities in the banking industry are growing with the help of technology. 1) What is the best way to make sure that once you have a job in banking, you can keep it or get another one? 2) What is a merger? 3) How does a merger affect bank employees?

Preparing for a Career in Finance

You can start preparing yourself now for a career in finance. While you're still in high school, take as many business-related courses as you can.

If you go to college, plan to take courses in business administration, economics, accounting, auditing, and finance. Keep in mind though that it is also important to take such subjects as psychology and sociology, speech, and English. You'll need good interpersonal skills to get along well with others.

If you're able to get a summer job as a bank teller, learn as much as you can about the various jobs in banking. Talk to your colleagues. Ask them what they like best and what they like least about their jobs. You can also ask people who work in banks about their jobs even if you don't work at a bank. As a bank customer and a potential employee, you're in a good position

Computer skills are very important in the field of banking. You can begin
learning many of these computer skills in high school.

to find out all kinds of information about banking.

Write to various financial organizations to find out about jobs that interest you. There are several listed at the end of this book. Read current business magazines and news magazines to keep on top of trends in banking and the economy. Read the classified section of the newspaper for job listings.

You can teach yourself to use a computer if you don't already know how by working with "user-friendly" programs. A lot of the computer software available today comes with an introduction that teaches you how to use it. And there is often a "help" feature to aid you when you don't understand something. It would be even better if you could take some classes in word processing and computer programming. Basic courses are offered at most community colleges and technical schools. In the future, almost all bank employees will use a computer to perform a large part of their work.

Writing a Résumé

In order to get a job in banking, including a summer job, you have to write a *résumé* and apply for the job. Your résumé should highlight your best points. A résumé is divided into four parts: personal information, education, work experience, and background experience. For more information about writing a great résumé, check your local library.

Applying for a Job

Once you have your résumé done and have collected a list of job openings, you are ready to *apply* for a job. Send your résumé along with a cover letter to the address listed. A *cover letter* briefly states where you heard about the job, that you would like to apply for it, and why you believe you are qualified for it. Mention that you will follow up with a phone call within a week or so. For more information, see the listing of books on the subject in the appendix called For Further Reading.

Interviews

An *interview* is a meeting between an employer and a potential employee. When interviewing for a position at a bank, take some time to think about what you want to say beforehand. You can practice in front of a mirror. Your goal is to appear comfortable and calm and to show that you are intelligent and knowledgable. But remember to be honest about what you don't know. Employers are usually more interested in a person who is willing to learn on the job than one who thinks she already knows everything there is to know.

Above all, be friendly. Bank employees work with people, not just money. It's important to show that you're a pleasant person to be around.

Questions to Ask Yourself

There are many things you can do to prepare for a career in banking and finance. 1) What are some courses you can take in high school that will help you later in your career? 2) What is a good method of discovering the positive and negative aspects of working in a bank? 3) What information should a résumé include?

Glossary

ABA American Banking Association.

assets What an individual or corporation owns.

auditor Person who examines the books and records of an organization to determine their accuracy and correctness.

CD Certificate of deposit.

CEO/CFO Chief Executive Officer/Chief Financial Officer: the two highest offices in a bank.

commercial bank Bank serving large institutions, such as schools and government.

consumer bank Bank serving small businesses and individuals.

controller Head of the accounting and budget departments of a financial institution. May also be called comptroller, treasurer, or financial manager.

counterfeit Fake.

CPA Certified Public Accountant.

credit analyst   Person who analyzes the strengths and weaknesses of an individual or a company to determine the financial risk of approving credit to them.

credit union   Nonprofit financial institution that specializes in loans and savings accounts, and is owned by its depositors.

direct deposit   Having your paycheck deposited directly into your savings or checking account.

estate   All of a person's assets.

financial company   Financial organization that loans money at a high interest rate.

in-service training   Seminars and courses taught by management at banks that are available to bank employees.

interest   Money paid for the use of borrowed money.

internship program   Working as an apprentice in a bank to learn about the various jobs involved in banking. An internship may be part of schoolwork.

merger   When two or more companies combine to form a single company.

money market account   Account in which money is invested, and from which a customer may draw funds using a check.

S & L   Savings and loan associations, which specialize in home mortgage loans as well as savings accounts.

transaction   The exchange of services or funds between a financial institution and an individual or company.

trust officer   Bank employee responsible for administering another person's property to that person's benefit.

For More Information

American Accounting Association
5717 Bessie Drive
Sarasota, FL 34233
(813) 921-7747

American Bankers Association (ABA)
1120 Connecticut Avenue NW
Washington, DC 20036
(202) 663-5382

American Institute of Banking (AIB)
1120 Connecticut Avenue NW
Washington, DC 20036
(202) 663-5153

American Money Management Association
(AMM)
5053 Fieldwood
Houston, TX 77056
(713) 965-0300

Credit Union Executives Society
P.O. Box 14167
Madison, WI 53714-0167
(800) 252-2664

Financial Manager's Society
8 South Michigan Avenue
Chicago, IL 60603
(312) 578-1300

Institute of Internal Auditors
249 Maitland Avenue
Altamonte Springs, FL 32701-4201
(407) 830-7600

Institute of Management Accountants
10 Paragon Drive
Montvale, NJ 07645-1760
(800) 638-4427

Mortgage Bankers Association of America
1125 15th Street NW
Washington, DC 20005
(202) 861-6500

For Further Reading

German-Grapes, Joan. *The Bank Teller's Handbook*. Chicago: Bankers Publishing Co., 1993.

Haddock, Patricia. *Careers in Banking and Finance*. New York: Rosen Publishing Group, 1990.

Morgan, Bradley. *Business and Finance Career Directory*. Detroit: Visible Ink Press, 1993.

Occupational Outlook Handbook. Washington, DC: U.S. Department of Labor, Bureau of Labor Statistics.

Paradis, Adrian, rev. by Philip Perry. *Opportunities in Banking Careers*. Lincolnwood, IL: VGM Career Horizons, 1993.

Resumes for Banking and Financial Careers. Lincolnwood, IL: UGM Career Horizons, 1993.

Ring, Trudy. *Careers in Finance*. Lincolnwood, IL: VGM Career Horizons, 1993.

Sumichrast, Michael, and Crist, Dean.

Opportunities in Financial Careers. Lincolnwood, IL: VGM Career Horizons, 1991.

Index

Acknowledgments
Special thanks to Betty Jo Bradstreet, a loan officer in a bank in
Augusta, Maine, as well as Mrs. Simpson's friend since high school;
Dewey Milby, Chief Financial Officer at a bank in Oklahoma as
well as Mrs. Simpson's brother-in-law; Clifton Clarke, a retired
senior agent with the Internal Revenue Service and a practicing
public accountant in Augusta, Maine, as well as Mrs. Simpson's
father.

About the Author
Carolyn Simpson teaches psychology at Tulsa Junior College in
Tulsa, Oklahoma. She has written numerous books on health-
related topics and career opportunities including *Careers in Social
Work, Careers in Medicine*, and *Careers Inside the World of Offices*.

Photo Credits: Cover, p. 29 © David W. Hamilton/Image Bank; p. 2 ©
Earl Dotter/Impact Visuals; pp. 7, 8, 10, 48 © Hazel Hankin/Impact
Visuals; p. 18 © Bill Hickey/Image Bank; p. 22 © Ted Kawalerski/Image
Bank; p. 24 © Peter Hendrie/Image Bank; p. 32 © Brett Froomer/Image
Bank; p. 39 © AP/Wide World Photos; p. 41 © Ansell Horn/Impact
Visuals; p. 44 © Williamson/ Edwards/Image Bank; p. 52 © Harvey
Finkle/Impact Visuals.

Design: Erin McKenna